THE BIG LITTLE BOOK

OF

RESILIENCE

How to bounce back from adversity
and lead a fulfilling life

First published 2015 in Pan by Pan Macmillan Australia Pty Ltd
1 Market Street, Sydney, New South Wales, Australia, 2000
Reprinted 2017, 2020
Text Copyright © Matthew Johnstone 2015
Illustration Copyright © Matthew Johnstone 2015

Cataloguing-in-Publication entry is available from the National Library of Australia
http://catalogue.nla.gov.au

ISBN: 978 1 742 61432 8

Design by Matthew Johnstone

Printed in China

The publishers and their respective employees or agents will not accept responsibility for injuries or damage occasioned to any person as a result of participation in the activities described in this book. It is recommended that individually tailored advice is sought from your healthcare professional.

PAN

Pan Macmillan Australia

Other bestselling books by the author

Matthew Johnstone is a passionate mental health and wellbeing advocate.
He's an author, illustrator, photographer, public speaker and
is also the creative director at the Black Dog Institute.
He lives in Sydney with his wife and two daughters.
To find out more please go to: **www.matthewjohnstone.com.au**

INNER PEACE

If you can start the day without coffee,

If you can always be cheerful, ignoring aches and pains,

If you can resist complaining and boring people with your troubles,

If you understand when your loved ones are too busy to give you any time,

If you can take criticism and blame without resentment,

If you can conquer tension without drugs,

If you can relax without alcohol,

If you can sleep without sleeping pills …

Well then, you're probably the family dog.

ANON

THE BIG LITTLE BOOK OF
RESILIENCE

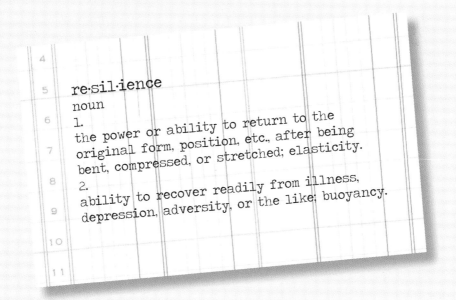

re·sil·ience
noun
1.
the power or ability to return to the
original form, position, etc., after being
bent, compressed, or stretched; elasticity.
2.
ability to recover readily from illness,
depression, adversity, or the like; buoyancy.

Written and Illustrated by
Matthew Johnstone

FOR MY WONDERFUL FAMILY
(BOTH IMMEDIATE AND EXTENDED)

My heartfelt thanks to Alex Craig,
Libby Turner and the staff at
Pan Macmillan Australia for believing in what I do.
To Pippa Masson and the staff at Curtis Brown
for their support, advice and guidance.
To the Black Dog Institute for the incredible work they do,
and being a continual source of inspiration and support.
And to everyone I've road-tested this book on,
thank you for your time and your valued feedback.
To lostandtaken.com, thank you for the textures once again.

Foreword

Watch any current affairs show on any given day and you're bound to see someone who has come out the other side of some bizarre, horrific, near-fatal, life-challenging event. For those affected, it's often a life-defining crossroad where everything changes, where they take stock of their lives and question what is truly important and alter their lives accordingly.

I feel I've had a pretty blessed life but along the way there have been a few defining moments.
I had a near-death experience following a massive asthma attack.
A friend and I were assaulted; he had his front teeth knocked out and I was chased by a guy with a knife who said he was going to kill me.
I stood a block from the World Trade Center when it came down.
And sporadically throughout my adult life, I have battled and thankfully overcome depression.
All these events were horrible, painful and frightening but in many ways they forged the person, the father, husband and friend that I am today. I wouldn't want to repeat any of the above but I wouldn't change anything either, mostly because I can't. Collectively, they opened my eyes to what I hold dear and value in my life.

Viktor Frankl, who miraculously survived three years in Nazi concentration camps including Auschwitz, wrote in his book *Man's Search for Meaning* that while we may have little control over events in our lives, what we have paramount control over is how we respond.

In many ways that's what this book is all about. We all have a story. We all have a journey, with both good and bad. We all have the ability to overcome difficulty and grow from the experience.

Whatever is going on in your life at this moment, I truly hope this big little book gives some inspiration, comfort, guidance and smiles. I also hope this finds you well wherever you may be.

Matthew Johnstone

PART I

To the uninitiated, resilience could be the secret ingredient in a fancy age-defying face cream.

In fact, resilience is all about developing a degree of flexibility and acceptance when it comes to life events.

It's not so much about what happens to you at the time of the event but how you respond or bounce back afterward.

Our lives, experiences, upbringings and families are all different, but it would be fair to say that most of us set out quietly hoping, and secretly expecting, to live a happy, successful and healthy life. This life would ideally be topped with some meaning and purpose, with a generous side order of solid and sustaining relationships.

BUT LIFE
DOESN'T ALWAYS
GO TO PLAN
OR PLAY FAIR.

This doesn't mean we should live with a sense of endless foreboding. It's an opportunity to live and experience each day

FULLY

One of the few sureties of life is that nothing is certain.

Peppered through our day-to-day continuum will
be curve balls, surprises and blindsides.
Not all of them are good, not all of them are bad.

These are the HILLS AND DALES OF LIFE.

SOME HILLS AND DALES OF LIFE

Love & Heartbreak

Success & Failure

Excitement & Boredom

Dreams & Realities

Health & Illness

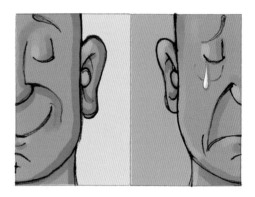

Happiness & Sadness

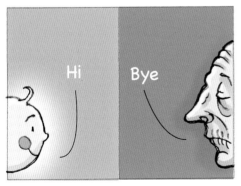

Life & Death

If we can learn to accept early on that life is going to be a mixed bag of positive and negative experiences, we're going to be much better equipped to deal with whatever life will inevitably throw at us down the track.

Another surety in life
is you cannot change the past.

You cannot change something
that may have happened to you.

You cannot change what someone
may have done to you.

You cannot change what you
may have done to others.

You cannot change your family,
as much as you might like to sometimes.

But with a degree of acceptance, understanding and insight, and the right help, we can alter perceptions, beliefs and outcomes of the less desirable events in our lives

FOR THE BETTER.

Accepting what we can and cannot change is one of the most important aspects of understanding resilience.

It's learning to work with and grow what's right in our lives while accepting, but not putting all our energy into, what's not.

Just because we stop physically growing doesn't mean we should stop growing intellectually, emotionally and spiritually.

Obviously you can change your weight, your hair colour, your wrinkles or the whiteness of your teeth but it's more of a challenge to change what lies behind the eyes.

When it comes to a lifetime of learned habits, rigid beliefs and the scar of life-altering events, we can always *evolve,*

knead,

enhance,

engage
and

improve.

Negative events can be terrible and painful. They can be life-changing and soul-destroying, both at the time and for some time after.

Yet nowhere does it state that the net effect should stain the rest of our lives, like a blighted tattoo.

Quite often the things we deem terrible can emerge as lateral teachers. The catch is that this wisdom can only be gleaned if we're prepared to learn and grow from the experience.

It's not that we should forget, it's just many choose not to learn or reflect on such events and thus become stuck in their own situation.

It's important to stress that resilience isn't necessarily gained only from going through something unfortunate. We can create strength and mental fortitude by going through tough positive experiences: climbing a mountain, completing a degree, having a child, running a marathon and so forth.

Tough doesn't always mean terrible, painful or tragic.

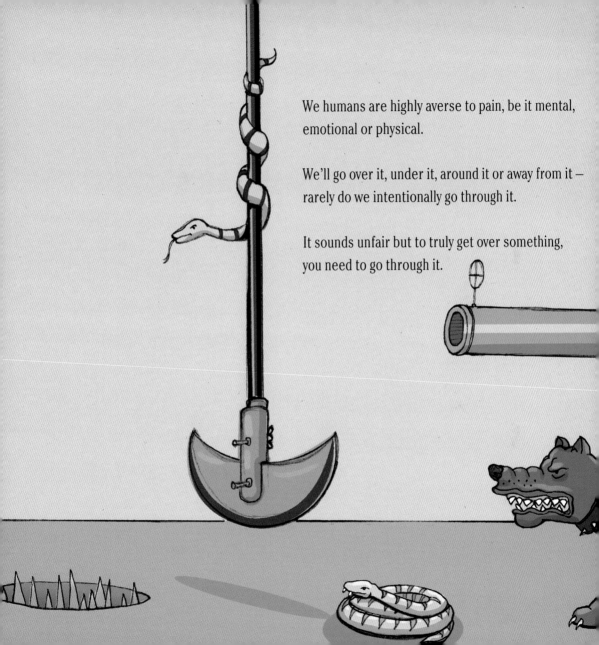

We humans are highly averse to pain, be it mental, emotional or physical.

We'll go over it, under it, around it or away from it — rarely do we intentionally go through it.

It sounds unfair but to truly get over something, you need to go through it.

When we fully embrace and try to understand
the situation and embark on a gentle and considered way
forward, we can come out the other side stronger for it.

We can become kinder, wiser, more understanding,
more compassionate and we can live with
a greater sense of purpose and meaning.

Humans are the consummate performers. We each invest vast amounts of energy into our 'show face'. This is the face we present to the world, the face we want others to see and to believe in. We could run power stations with the amount of energy we invest in our show faces.

Why do we do this? Is it shame, stigma, ego, not wanting to complain, not wanting to appear weak, not wanting to be a burden?

If we took half the energy that we invest into covering something up and used it to actually understand and heal the wound, we could move through it and get on with life a lot quicker.

When it comes to being authentic, vulnerable and speaking from the heart, we have to look beyond the perceived dangers of doing so.

Our history, fears, thoughts and distorted beliefs can hold us hostage in our own minds. We have to be brave and focus on the freedom of being our true selves.

At some stage, there has to be a sort of surrender to the process, the situation and the outcome. If we are talking to the right people, getting the right help, and doing the things that bring wellbeing into our lives

then that is all we can do.

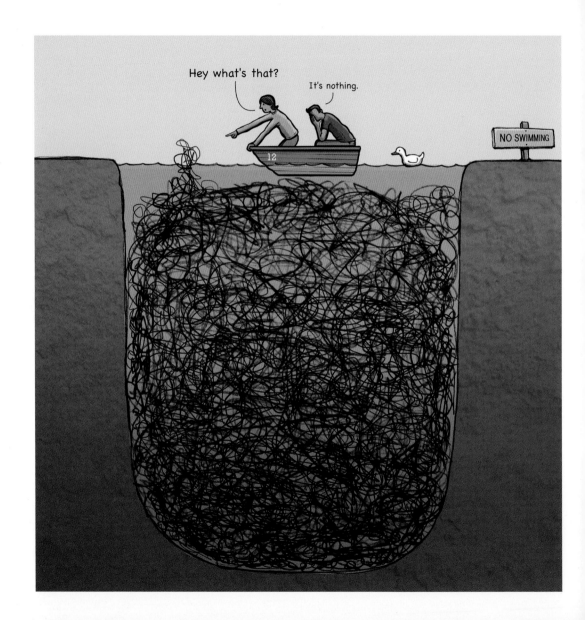

When faced with any kind of adversity in life, we often look for the quick fix, the get-out-of-jail-free card, and when that's not forthcoming, we will swallow the problem into the vast lake of our being, hoping to suppress its shock and awe.

This lake has immense capacity. We can keep turning up with our toxic swill and dumping it in there for a long time.

The problem is that the lake has a bottom and if we're not processing, recycling and mopping up, the quagmire will overflow. This can not only affect us mentally and physically but can also impact those around us.

WHERE TO FROM HERE?

Do we stay down or get up?

Do we remain a victim or become a survivor?

Are we weakened or strengthened?

Do we stay stuck or do we move forward?

Can we make a negative situation a turning point for change?

Others can and will help along the way but in the end it's really all up to you.

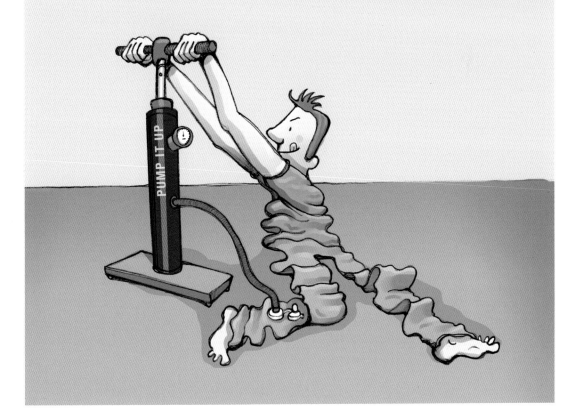

The first step is to acknowledge that there is a problem:

- I am not coping.
- I have a mental health issue.
- I have a physical impairment.
- I have a substance addiction.
- I have been abused.
- I am anxious.
- I find no joy in anything ...

It requires total honesty with yourself and then with others.

Although the first step of recovery or seeking help can be the biggest and most daunting, it is also the most important.

There will inevitably be many steps and stumbles that follow but from this moment on, with the right amount of determination, perseverance and help, it's a matter of continually moving forward and upward, one step at a time.

I OWN

MY

PROBLEMS.

MY PROBLEMS DON'T OWN ME.

A vitally important virtue is patience. In this world of everything being instant, we expect the same when it comes to our difficulties.

The secret is to take the problem and break it down into manageable chunks.

During this mining process, there are gems to be found.

These gems can be love and support we didn't realise we had. An inner strength we never knew existed. A new and improved way of expressing ourselves. There can be valuable insights and understandings about ourselves and others.

It seems counterintuitive but there is real strength to be found in learning how to be vulnerable, authentic and to speak from a place of truth.

This can prove challenging because we've had a lifetime of building up our show face, our defences, sleight of hand and *trompe l'oeils*.

When we speak from the heart and learn to be genuine, there is no shadow in which we can hide. There is freedom in this and when we share, we allow others to do the same.

Those important people in our lives will generally respond favourably to emotional honesty and will help as best they can.

If they don't, perhaps it's because it hits too close to the bone of their own experiences, shortcomings or fears.

Another vitally important aspect of resilience is developing a sense of compassion for yourself and what you've been through.

Self-compassion isn't being self-indulgent or soft. It's not about feeling sorry for yourself, it's about <u>not</u> beating yourself up for feeling bad, feeling pain or not coping.

No one persecutes us mentally and emotionally more than ourselves.

Self-compassion is about being gentle and kind with yourself as you would an infant, the elderly or someone you love. It's also about doing good things for yourself like exercise, meditation, eating well and helping others.

When we become compassionate to our own needs, it's only natural that we then become compassionate and empathetic to others, which is always a good thing.

It is perfectly

K...

... not to feel

K

The trick is not getting stuck.

When it comes to the way that we think of ourselves and what may currently be going on in our lives, it's very important to discern fact from fiction. Our thoughts are phenomenally powerful. They can become intrusive, repetitive, obsessive and very persuasive.

The movies we play in our minds can be IMAX in size, with Dolby surround sound, 3D and impressive production values.
These movies are often horror films, screening in the small hours of the morning.

Yet as real and convincing as these movies can be, you have to remind yourself that ...

... THOUGHTS *are* NOT

FACTS

Take a moment to consider what this means and then tattoo it onto your brain.

Browse any self-help section in a book store and you'll find plenty of books with an emphasis on having happy thoughts, positive mantras and creating lovely manifestations.

There's nothing intrinsically wrong with this but rather than avoiding unpleasant thoughts, feelings and fears, why not try embracing them? Why not try and understand why you're having them in the first place?

Don't sweep them under the rug, don't suppress them, don't drown them with alcohol and other forms of self-medication.

FEAR

Take them on, challenge them at their own game.

Say 'do your worst!' because by this stage, they probably have.
If they are thoughts that frighten you, then turn them into something
worthy of a cartoon, make them comical. Change the story and you can
change the outcome.

If you really don't feel in control of your thoughts or feelings, talk to
a mental health professional.

FEARless

One of the ways we can address our worrying thoughts and fears is to make room for some 'worry time'. Allow five to ten minutes every other day, writing down everything you deem frown-inducing.

When the list is complete, take a moment to quietly read it through then take small pleasure with some ceremony in destroying what you've written. Screw it up, rip it up, stamp on it or pop it on the BBQ.

Once done, literally leave your worries behind and get on with your day, knowing that you've drawn a mental line in the sand.
This exercise is not intended to solve all your problems; however the very process of acknowledging your issues is highly cathartic and allows more space for positive solutions.

IF YOU'RE STRUGGLING, THERE'S NO SHAME IN ASKING FOR HELP.

THE ONLY REAL SHAME IS MISSING OUT ON LIFE.

Having a shoulder to cry on can be helpful, but if you're not coping emotionally or mentally, or you're facing a more serious life event, that person may not be well-equipped or qualified to deal with the issue at hand. Which is why it can be worthwhile talking to a complete stranger in the form of a psychiatrist, a psychologist or a counsellor; they are all trained to help when we're under mental duress.

They can help us reframe the way we think. They can change the way we perceive a problem. They can help us challenge negative beliefs and can give us useful cognitive tools to help manage most situations and feelings.

It can be beneficial to educatc yourself about the different roles in mental health and to understand different styles of treatment and therapy. In doing so, it won't feel like such a mystery and will give you a greater sense of control over your situation.

When considering a mental health professional, think of it like shopping for a good pair of shoes; it should feel like the right fit. If you're going to tell a stranger your problems, you should feel like you're in a place of sanctuary.

They are not there to be your friend, they are not there to judge, to criticise or make you do things you don't want to do.

It's a professional relationship where empathy, support and understanding combined with a solid plan toward recovery and wellbeing should all make for a positive outcome.

How to Build, Develop and Nurture Resilience

A lot of what you're about to read will seem obvious or even perhaps a bit twee, but all the things that help to build resilience and wellbeing are those that we constantly neglect to do for ourselves.
To live a mentally and physically robust life is all about 'life management' and the discipline to do the things that make us feel good and give us strength.

Often you hear *'I don't have time to exercise, to meditate, to eat well'*.
The net result of this attitude is that people only stop when they're too sick to carry on. So make time. Do it for yourself. Do it for others.
Prevention is, after all, the greatest cure.

PART II

It has been clinically proven that regular exercise is as effective for treating mild to moderate depression and anxiety as antidepressants.

Exercise can make a profound difference on our outlook. It boosts our mood, it helps us to lose weight, it can fight myriad diseases and it can also improve our sleep.

Around 30 minutes of physical activity daily is recommended.

This does not mean that we have to run marathons, swim oceans or live at the gym. We can have have our regular exercise like walking, running, swimming etc. interspersed with incidental activities such as getting off the bus a couple of stops early, taking the stairs instead of the lift, walking to get (a healthy) lunch instead of sitting at our desks, or treating housework as a workout.

Sweat out the bad stuff so you can experience more of the good.

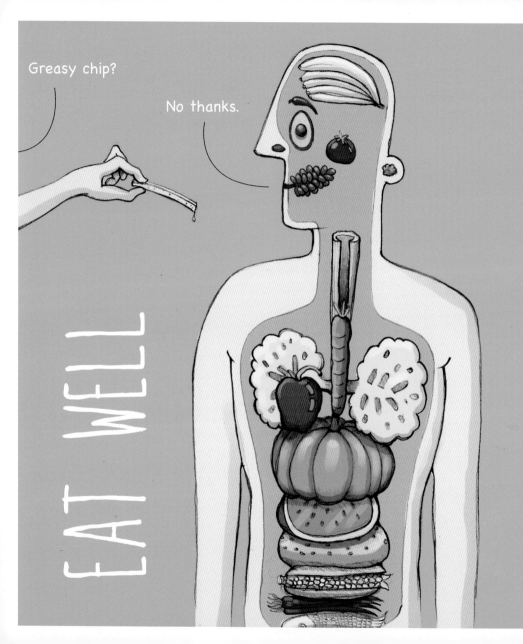

Quite often we eat in accordance with how we're feeling. We tend to eat badly when we're stressed, bored, lonely or even celebrating. This 'comfort food' can make us feel like rubbish.

If you want to know just how well you can feel, try going on a detox for four to six weeks. Don't be surprised if you feel a bit lousy in the beginning; your body will be howling for what it craves. There may be headaches and feelings of agitation but they should pass in the first week or so. After that you'll start to feel more energised, focused, motivated, happy and you'll begin to look better too.

By removing the usual suspects of caffeine, sugar, red meat, alcohol, wheat and dairy, you'll be nudged toward a diet of fruit, vegetables, whole grains, fish, chicken and dairy alternatives.

Don't think of it as a 'diet', but as the ultimate self-compassionate experiment that will do you a world of good. Your palate will simplify to appreciate more delicate and subtle flavours. You'll realise how much of society is based around passive addictions and habitual behaviour.

How often do you hear, I can't do without *'my morning coffee'*, *'my glass of wine with dinner'*, *'my evening choccy'*? Just remove that little word *'can't'* from your vocabulary and realise you *'can'* do without these foods.

Once you discover how well you can feel, you will gravitate toward a fresh and natural diet that will hopefully become *'most of the time'* rather than *'some of the time'*.

Put some time into researching the best approach for you, and drink lots of water while you're at it.

Cocaine can give us confidence.
Ecstasy can make us lovey-dovey.
Marijuana can chill us out.
Alcohol helps us to relax and socialise.

These, and the other potential effects of drugs and alcohol, can be quite enticing to anyone who is stressed, depressed, anxious, bored, feeling peer pressure or has a desire to experiment. They can all deliver on their promises but at a cost; often a big cost.

It's the cost of damage inflicted on the brain and the long-term effect on mental health. It's the cost of addiction and the overall cost in treatment and loss of productivity to society.

Alcohol, the most publicly condoned of the lot, is responsible for the lion's share of assaults, hospitalisations, DUIs and vandalism, and many health problems.

The biggest reason people abuse drugs or drink alcohol to excess is that they see them as the panacea to their problems – they blunt, diffuse or suspend pain and reality. In the end, this solution can become the biggest problem of all.

Do yourself, your brain and society a massive favour by getting more out of life, not more 'out of it'.

When good sleep goes, so does everything that depends on it; your mood, your memory, your ability to get things done and to focus, and it makes you feel generally lousy. Having rubbish sleep is like pouring alcohol on your cornflakes: it's just not a good way to start the day.

Bad sleep not only affects us cognitively but if we continually have bad sleep, it can increase obesity, heart disease and diabetes – and it can shorten your life expectancy.

People need different amounts of sleep but the golden rule is around seven to eight hours of decent sleep per night to function properly.

Invest in a really good bed and bedding; you spend over a third of your life there. Try to avoid caffeine, alcohol, exercise, stimulating movies or video games right before bed. Have a bath. Have a warm drink. Read a book. Dim the lights. Listen to relaxing music. Write lists of concerns prior to sleep. Learn deep breathing relaxation techniques.

MAKE YOUR BED A SACRED PLACE.

Most of us breathe incorrectly. Our breathing is wonderfully automated, so we don't give it much thought but perhaps we should. Most of us breathe as if our lungs end just below our collarbones: short, shallow, quick breaths that nourish very little.

In simple terms, if oxygen is life, we're not getting the most out of it.

Breathing deeply increases our energy, creates better mental clarity and helps our organs and blood to detox.

To see how we should breathe, look to a baby. They breathe naturally and deeply, into their stomachs while expanding their rib cage.

The next time you feel stressed or angry, remove yourself from the situation, find a quiet place and take five to ten slow deep breaths right down to your navel. Put your hand on your stomach and make it rise.
Breathe in fully for four beats, hold for two beats, then exhale slowly until your lungs feel empty. Repeat until you feel calm and nourished.

It could be said that social media is amplifying society's level of narcissism. There is a lot more *'I'* and *'me'*, less *'you'*, *'us'* and *'we'*. This 'selfie culture' can also lead to a sense of isolation, which is another good reason to make life less about you and more about others.

Connect to something bigger than yourself. It could be your faith, your family, your job, your community, the environment, a cause, a sports team and so forth.

When we give of ourselves, life gives back. We feel fulfilled, connected and have a greater sense of purpose.

Do and believe in things that make you glow, that bring you joy, that feel effortless.

It's easy to say *'who am I in this world of billions?'* but everyone has their role to play, everyone has something they can offer, everyone can be of service, everyone can create positive change.

Trying something new can push us out of our comfort zones, which in many ways is the very reason to do it. Attempting new things can be daunting but they can get us off our butts, open us up to new experiences, new skills, new ways of thinking and people with similar interests.

We can discover facets of ourselves that we never knew existed. It's also a wonderful way to connect with the greater community and to feel a part of something. Not only can this be fun but it can bring fulfilment and a new-found enthusiasm for life.

So challenge yourself by joining a club, a group, a community project, a support group or volunteer for something you're passionate about.

Apparently those who learn another language are less likely to develop dementia. So trying something *nouveau* clearly has major mental health benefits too.

To evolve, get involved.

HAVE A DIGITAL DETOX

ONLINE

OFFLINE

Computers, tablets and smartphones are wonderful examples of human ingenuity, endeavour and achievement.

Useful, smart and, at times, indispensable but next time you're waiting for a plane, train or bus, do a quick tally of how many people are on devices.

Emails, texts, social media and gaming all keep us from what's going on around us and connecting with one another. It's an addictive form of stimulation and diversion.

It seems we are losing our ability to sit, to observe, to daydream, to converse, to be bored. When the brain is constantly kept busy by bright shiny things, it becomes increasingly difficult to quieten it down.

Modern-day self-esteem comes externally from how many 'friends' we have or how many 'likes' and 'retweets' we acquire.

Playdates have become kids leaning over tablets or gaming devices.

Smartphones have become uninvited guests at dinner tables.

Workplaces have become quieter because it's easier to type than it is to walk and talk.

Technology is by no means bad, but sometimes to tune in to life, we need to 'turn off' more often.

ff

Music is the season for our moods. It is the dog-eared bookmark of our lives.
It is a force that motivates us to tap, hum, sing and dance.
It can make the hairs on the backs of our necks stand in ovation.
It is something that connects us all on a tribal and heartfelt level.

Music is the most wonderful, intangible human endeavour that has no reason
for being other than to bring a sense of:

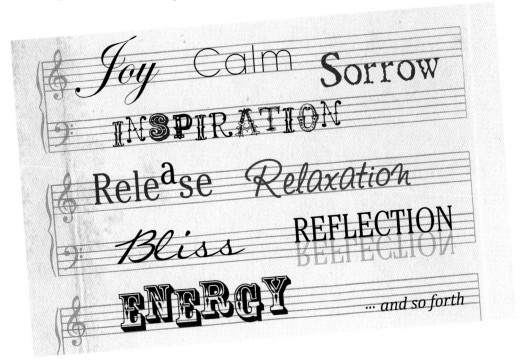

See some, play some, listen to some.

Keep GOOD Company

As you get older you begin to realise that life is short. Get the most out of it by being around people who make you feel good while making a conscious and deliberate effort to extricate yourself from those who are toxic, make you feel bad or enable you in activities that are not good for you.

A person of positive influence should be a good listener, be interested in you and your life (as you should be for them). They should be supportive of you and never put you down. Someone you share values with, can laugh with, and where conversations flow naturally.

People who are cynical, sarcastic, destructive or full of contempt bring no added value and simply drain what is good out of life, namely yours.

Deep down we all know what sort of person we are and how we behave around others. If you tilt toward the negative side of the scales, it's never too late to change, to get help and improve this aspect of yourself. When you hurt others you hurt yourself. So start by becoming your own best friend and go from there.

If someone has done the wrong thing by you, one of the best (and sometimes toughest) things you can do is find a place in your heart for forgiveness. When you forgive you can let go; when you let go, you can move forward.

This by no means condones what they have done. You don't have to see them again. You don't even have to tell them.

Forgiveness simply allows you to get on with your life.

You can tell your story over and over, and you'll probably get the same validating *'how terrible!'* response, but in the end anger, resentment and contempt all have a terribly corrosive effect on the soul.

As you ponder forgiveness, consider what may have happened in that person's life that made them who they are and how it may have forged what they did.

If it is you that has done the wrong thing, forgive yourself; we are more than the sum total of our mistakes. Learn from the mistake and do the right thing and make amends for your actions. It is never too late.

Never understimate the power of a meaningful apology, nor the power of being able to accept one.

Do the Stuff You Love

Why do avid gardeners passionately do what they do?

They are outside, they receive vitamin D from the sun. It's physical work, there's a connection to the earth. There's great planning, forecasting and working with the seasons. Then there's a return on time and labour invested in the way of a beautiful garden that provides flowers, fruits or vegetables. These gifts not only feed, but can bring a real sense of joy, pride and achievement.

If you don't think you have an activity in your life that brings you these sorts of benefits, think back to an activity you did as a child that could make time stand still. Where the effort for this pastime was akin to riding a bike with the wind behind your back. There were no thoughts of yesterday or tomorrow, just a laser-beam intensity directed to the project at hand. We might call this bliss, a halcyon bubble or our happy place.

If you haven't integrated an aspect, or an interpretation of this activity into your adult life, ask yourself: why not?

Make a time in your day, week or month that is all about you and the thing that makes your heart sing and your mind smile.

It can be the difference between doing life and living it.

Sitting in silence or becoming more observant of the current moment tends to be one of the more challenging wellbeing activities. It goes against the very nature of our overly active and increasingly stimulated brains.

There are myriad mental and physical benefits to learning meditation and mindfulness. To start with, it opens up more space for creativity and productivity while instilling a quiet calm that can weather any storm. We are also more engaged with what we're doing and who we're with.

It's not about having <u>no</u> thoughts, it's more about not engaging with, reacting to or chasing them. It's about quietly observing, without judgement.
It's about quietening your mind, one breath at a time.

People often say *'I tried meditation once and I just couldn't do it!'* It's a bit like saying *'I went for a run once and when I came back I wasn't fit!'*. Just like exercise and eating well, it's so worth pursuing.

BIG THANKS

FOR LITTLE THINGS

Rather than focussing on everything that is wrong or missing in your life, try looking at what is right, then practise thinking and saying *'thanks for that'*.

We shouldn't hold out on our gratitude for the bigger house, the fancier car, the pay rise; it should be for the unexpected hug, cup of tea, hanging out with a good friend, a fine day, an unexpected compliment, a drawing by a child and so forth.

Think of yourself as an 'Appreciation Collector', the more you collect, the bigger the collection; the bigger the collection, the greater the value we find in life. It all adds up.

Gratitude is simply the palette that paints a better picture of life.

Dame Grace Manyblessings *Sir Gracias Thanksalot*

The majority of us are capable of listening and talking but ask yourself, do you do both of these activities well?

Being a great communicator is a skill worth learning.

There's an art to being able to listen to where someone is coming from without instantly going on the defensive, without having to constantly jump in or 'one-up' with a story of your own or refraining from the need to tell them what they should do. Being contemplative, considered and thoughtful in any form of conversation is a form of personal mastery. As is being able to clearly articulate what you may be going through.

There's nothing worse than being talked at or not being listened to.

Just as there's nothing greater than thinking *we could have talked all night*.

SET YOURSELF A GOAL

If you have a degree of discontent or feel stuck about how your life is panning out, having a goal is a good way to change the current trajectory.

Goals help bring out your true potential. They create energy, focus and they force you to live your life more consciously.

Everyone has a dream, a novel, an invention, a movie idea and so often these are realised by others because they 'did' rather than pondered.

Often we begin to hatch a plan and then think of a million reasons why it couldn't happen in the same thought bubble.

So ask yourself, if time and money were no object what would you love to do?

The answer could be a massive hairy, scary, bodacious idea or could be something relatively simple. Whether it's 10 steps or 1000 steps to that goal, take that first step. Make a pledge with yourself that each day, each week, each month, you will do something small, medium and large toward your goal. You have nothing to lose but the time you spend doing something that doesn't fulfil you.

Talk to people, get advice, find a mentor, be passionate.

If it doesn't work out, you will have extended yourself, learnt new skills, met new people and perhaps discovered other ideas worth exploring.

If it does work out, the first question you'll ask is *'why didn't I do this sooner?'*.

REWARD
THYSELF

When major birthdays roll around we often find ourselves asking where did all the time go? Busy work, family and social schedules tend to make time fly and it only seems to go faster as we get older.

So step on the brakes every once in a while and take a tally of all the things you've done that have made you and possibly others proud. Recognise and honour your path, your progress and take pride in what you've achieved, both big and small.

It could be overcoming a difficulty, it could be your kids, your garden, a project at work, a ship made out of tooth picks.

Whatever it is, visualise a squadron of jets flying overhead, spurred on by a huge brass band and a spectacular fireworks display while graciously saying *'I did that!'*.

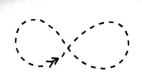

No matter what adverse life experience you've
been through, there is incredible catharsis to be found in
the telling of your story and what you've learnt from it.

Joining a support group, volunteering for a cause,
writing a book or a blog lets people who are maybe
going through something similar know that they are
not alone, flawed, failed or doomed.

When you give of yourself, life gives back.

*Help yourself by
helping others.*

Final Thoughts

Appreciate little things.

Nurture compassion.

Find joy in the moment.

Learn to quiet your mind.

Strive for wellbeing.

Speak from the heart.

Grow from adversity.

Always hold onto hope.

Live with love.

END ON AN UP

There are an incredible number of inspiring people who have overcome amazing odds. Here are just a few for you to google should you need some inspiration.

Bethany Hamilton

Douglas Bader

Kris Carr

Helen Keller

Viktor Frankl

Mark Zupan

Malala Yousafzai

Nick Vujicic

Candace Lightner

Turia Pitt

Stephen Hawking

Bruce & Denise Morcombe

RESOURCES*

MENTAL HEALTH
www.blackdoginstitute.org.au
www.mycompass.org.au
www.lifeline.org.au
www.beyondblue.org.au
www.biteback.org.au (teen)
www.headspace.org.au (teen)
www.au.reachout.com (teen)
www.kidshelpline.com.au (kids / teen)

BETTER SLEEP
www.sleep.org.au
www.sleephealthfoundation.org.au

FOOD / NUTRITION
www.thefoodcoach.com.au
www.thewholepantryapp.com
www.bodyandsoul.com.au
www2.drjoanna.com.au

RELATIONSHIPS
www.relationships.org.au
www.jeanhailes.org.au (women)
www.mensline.org.au (men)

DRUGS AND ALCOHOL
www.aa.org.au
www.na.org.au
www.alcohol.gov.au
www.shadetreatment.com
www.hellosundaymorning.org
www.talktofrank.com (UK)

MEDITATION AND MINDFULNESS
www.actmindfully.com.au
www.smilingmind.com.au
www.wildmind.org

EXERCISE
www.physicalactivityaustralia.org.au
7 minute workout (app)
Couch to 5K (running app)
Zombies, Run! (running app)

GET INVOLVED
www.actbelongcommit.org.au
www.australiancharityguide.com

*There are so many wonderful (mostly free) resources out there, this is just the tip of the iceberg.

NOTES

NOTES

NOTES